Just Stop anc Think

Helping children plan to improve their own behaviour

by
Fiona Wallace

Book Cover by
Philippa Drakeford

Printed in England by The Book Factory, London N1 4RS

Contents

Acknowledgement

A big thank you to the pupils of Baverstock School who have
allowed me to help them improve their own behaviour.

Introduction

Children who struggle with their behaviour, just like those who struggle with an academic task such as learning to read or perform maths calculations, need extra, regular, structured help from adults in school to build on the skills already mastered. With both learning and behaviour difficulties, time should be spent with the pupil looking at the skills they already have and agreeing targets for the future. Just as when working to improve an academic skill, a structured programme of support needs to be put in place to teach the appropriate behaviours. This book provides a ready-made set of materials, for staff working with pupils who are experiencing difficulty in school with their behaviour:

* to look at the current situation
* to explore the range of possible ways forward
* to draw up an action plan and record progress.

This book could be used in conjunction with two earlier publications, **Not you again...!** and **What else can I do with you?**, which focus on improving or removing particular playground and classroom behaviours. However, in contrast to the materials in the first two books, those in Just stop and think are not linked to any specific problem behaviour. They can be used for a wide range of difficulties, from the acting-out behaviours so familiar to teachers of late primary, early secondary pupils, to the more withdrawn behaviours shown by some pupils under great emotional stress. Some of the principles which guided the development of all three books are listed below:

* Adults can help children improve their behaviour without resorting to punishment or to strategies based on lost learning opportunities.

* Staff should be able to deal effectively with a child in trouble without automatically attributing blame to the child or their actions.

* Children should take responsibility for their actions....both those that get them into trouble and those that they can take to change their behaviour for the better.

* No child should be written-off as beyond help and neither is any child perfect. There is always the chance to learn new skills and strengthen existing positive behaviours and relationships.

* Resources for teachers must be easy to use. These sheets only need copying and this can be done freely within the purchasing establishment.

Before you start

A solution-focussed, brief therapy model of helping reminds us that any step in the right direction, however small, is worth encouraging and that the 'client' always has at least part of their solution available to them. It also reminds us not to take control and direct the way in which a difficulty could be resolved. Our aim should be to help the pupil find their own solution rather than to become an expert on their problem. When using these materials our role is to support the pupil in exploring the situation they find themselves in. Instead of dwelling on past problems, we should try to keep the focus on learning from what has happened and putting those lessons into practise for future improvement. We should try to help pupils see what they already know about their difficulties and potential solutions, then guide them in opening up possibilities that will help them move forward. Above all, we must remember that it is the problem that needs solving, not the pupil !

The language we use when working through these sheets is important if we are to remain as advisors and not become directors. It is very hard not to slip into the 'I'm the expert on your behaviour' role. It is hard not to launch into saying things like

"You need to..." "You should try..." "If I were you..."

Many of the things we would usually say can be re-phrased to fit a solution-focussed approach. Try versions of these:

   * What would you like to change?
   * What is different since we last met?
   * When does the problem happen less / not happen? Why?
   * How will you know when things are starting to get better?
   * What will other people notice as things improve?
   * What do you think you should do more of?
   * If this is the worst it can be what are you doing to keep yourself going?
   * What would people notice if the problem went away?
   * What would they / you be doing that was different?
   * What have you learned that might help you?
   * How will I know if this session has been useful to you?

The pupils' answers to questions like these will begin to open up a range of possible ways forward. But, before coming up with a list of things to do, it is important to help pupils reflect on where they are now and where they would like to be so that they can form a realistic view of the progress to be made. Scaling questions are useful here. For example:

   * On a scale of 1 (the pits) to 10 (perfection!) where are you now?
   * Why are you at that point?
   * How will you know when you have moved one point (or more) up?
   * What point of the scale do you want to be at?

Once a realistic point to aim for has been agreed then we can begin to help the pupil plan how best to move in that direction, using their own suggestions for progress markers along the way.

The book is divided into 2 sections. Section 1 encourages pupils to look at the situation they find themselves in by considering:

* observations of their own behaviour
* others' point of view
* how the future might look
* the range of choices for action
* potential help and pitfalls.

Section 2 gives a range of different ways to help pupils plan a series of actions. The emphasis is on doing something next lesson, today and not on spending hours thinking and prevaricating about taking the first few difficult steps. Remember any step in the right direction is worth celebrating and encouraging.

However much staff would like to spend unlimited time helping pupils analyse a situation, learn from it and plan a way forward, time in the busy school day is going to be limited. A 15-20 minute session should be enough to work through each of the sheets. Some may need more than one session if there is a suggested activity linked to the sheet. All could have a follow up session to help the pupil review their progress and plan what to do next but this may need to be the pupil's choice.

Your time together might go something like this:

Hello, how are you? Establish a rapport with the pupil to help them feel you are on their side, at least for the next 20 minutes!

What's new? Ask what has happened that is helpful since you agreed to meet ... last met ... the outburst in class... The idea is to help the pupil see that they can make changes by themselves, already have part of the solution to their predicament... and that you do not need to make the changes for them.

Moving on. This will be the main work of the session using one of the sheets. If possible develop ideas suggested by the pupil that have already begun to work for them.

Winding up. Remind yourself and the pupil of the key points of the session, in particular the action plan. Agree if, and when, you need to meet again.

Record keeping

Those pupils for whom sessions using these resources are appropriate will usually be on the 'Code of Practice.' A record will need to be kept of help given and plans made. The pupil should keep their sheet as a reminder of issues discussed and the things they are going to do. If the pupil wishes to put his or her name on the sheet then OK but this should not be insisted upon. If the work is lost then it should not draw attention to the pupil when found. However staff will need to keep some record of the session, perhaps towards a review of the pupil's Individual Behaviour Plan (IBP). The record sheet at the end of this section (page 8) can be freely photocopied and allows staff to note the issues raised, the plans made and any reminders for areas to explore in future meetings.

Be creative with the pupils you work with! Use these materials in any way you feel would be helpful to the pupil.

Further reading

The further reading suggested in Not you again and What else can I do with you? provides an excellent starting point for this book list too. The full references for these two companions to this book are

Fiona Wallace and Diane Caesar.
Not you again...!
Lucky Duck 1995

Fiona Wallace
What else can I do with you?
Lucky Duck 1998

Those of you who want to know more about solution -focused brief therapy might like to read

E George, C Iveson and H Ratner
Problem to Solution - Brief Therapy with Individuals and Families
Brief Therapy Press 1999

Practical applications of this theory can be seen in

B Stringer and M Mall
Anger Management With Children
Questions Publishing Company 1999

T Rae
Confidence, assertiveness and self esteem: for secondary pupils
Lucky Duck 2001

Just Stop and Think

Worksheet title   ....   Page number   ....

Pupil   ....

Staff   ....   Date of session......................

Key points from this session

Actions for staff (What? Who? When?)

Issues for exploration at a future session

Date, time and place of next session (If needed)

Review of progress made in this area

Section 1

Observations by Young People of their Own Behaviour

The more you tramp on a cow pat the bigger it gets!"

In other words… don't make your problems worse than they already are.

What do you do that makes your problems worse? Perhaps you answer back or sigh loudly or use a sarcastic tone of voice.

If you stopped doing these things how do you think your teacher would feel?

How would you feel?

What would your friends think?

Person spec.

When jobs are advertised a *person specification* is written to make it clear what kind of person is needed.

What kind of person do you need to be to fill the job of 'successful pupil at school'?

Job Title   Successful pupil   full/~~part~~ time
                 at school   ~~temporary~~/permanent

Essential characteristics, skills and knowledge.

Desirable characteristics, skills and knowledge

I Will

Try to ....

.... (Target)

Keep trying for .... (Time Scale)

Keep this chart to show how well I am doing

Date	Oh dear! ☹	Nearly 😐	Hurrah 🙂	Comments

Watch it

I am going to circle the next number each time I

....

....

....

I will start .... and finish ....

I guess I will circle up to about number ....

1	2	3	4	5	6	7	8	9	10
11	12	13	14	15	16	17	18	19	20
21	22	23	24	25	26	27	28	29	30
31	32	33	34	35	36	37	38	39	40
41	42	43	44	45	46	47	48	49	50

Now I know what I am doing,

I am going to change by ....

....

A... B... C...

Over the next few days look carefully at what happens around the times you get into trouble. Fill in this chart to help you focus on how to make some changes.

When did it happen date/lesson/time?	**What** A was happening **Around** you at the time?	**What** B was your **Behaviour** and what did you do?	**What** C happened next? **Consequences**...

Time line

- How did you get here?
- What are the milestones along the way?
- Are there any places where you feel you might have taken a wrong turn?

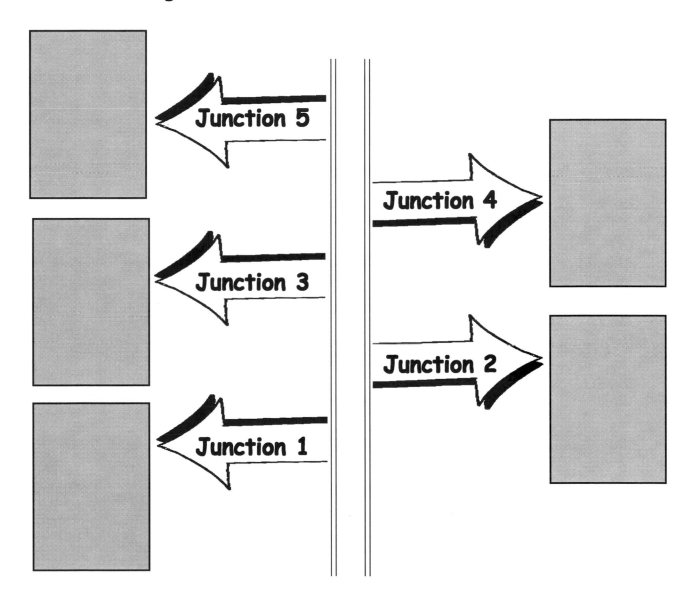

Fill in the signposts along the road to show the significant events for your journey up to today.

How low can you go?

Think about a time when things were worse than now, when things were as bad as they could be ..... the pits.

Now, before you get too depressed, think about what you have done to get yourself out of the pit to where you are now.

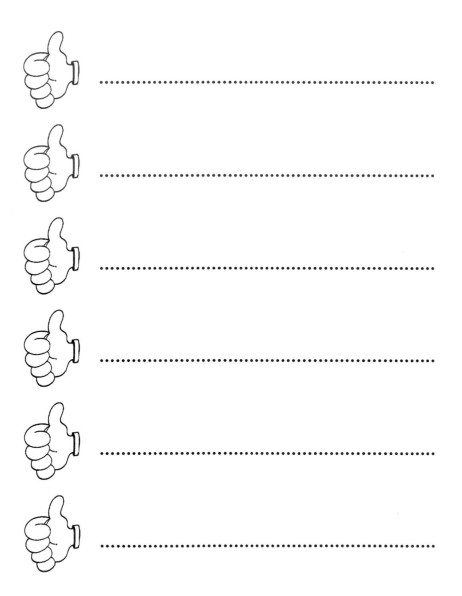

Which of these things could you do more of / better / for longer to move still further ahead.

CV

When people apply for new jobs they send a CV to describe themselves and say what they have done and what they are good at. Sometimes they say why they should have the job. They give the name of someone who will say they will be good at the job. This is called a reference.

Write a Cv for the job of pupil in your school

Name   DOB

My education so far:

Skills I have for the job:

Hobbies and interests:

My targets for the future in this job:

A reference can be obtained from:

Archaeological dig

Archaeologists dig back through time to find out what life was like thousands of years ago. Can you think back just a short while to a time when things were better for you in school.

What can you learn from that time that will help you get on better now?

Things were better when....

At that time I did more of these things....

And I did less of these things....

It would help me now if I did more...

And did less...

You're a star

Everyone has lots of good points. What have you done well recently to try to improve your behaviour? Write these things on the star.

What do you need to do to make your star shine even more brightly?

Considering the Views of Other People

If the cap fits....

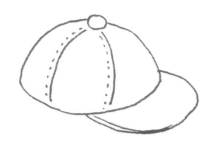

What do others say about you?	What would you prefer them to say?

Are there any statements on the left which you feel pleased about?

Which of the statements on the right is the one you most want to come true?

Fly on the Wall

Imagine you are a fly on the wall at school watching what goes on.

- ◆ What do different people think of your behaviour?
- ◆ What do they think you could do to improve?
- ◆ Why do they think you get into trouble?

Use the chart below to record what other people might think as they buzz round school watching you. You might imagine the flies to be some of these:

Friends	Girls
Teachers	Boys
Other adults in school	Younger pupils
Family	Older pupils

Put three names and what they think by each fly.

....

....

....

....

....

....

Opposites

Think of some words that describe your behaviour and note them down in the boxes on the left hand end of each line.

Now put the opposite of each word in the box at the right hand end of each line.

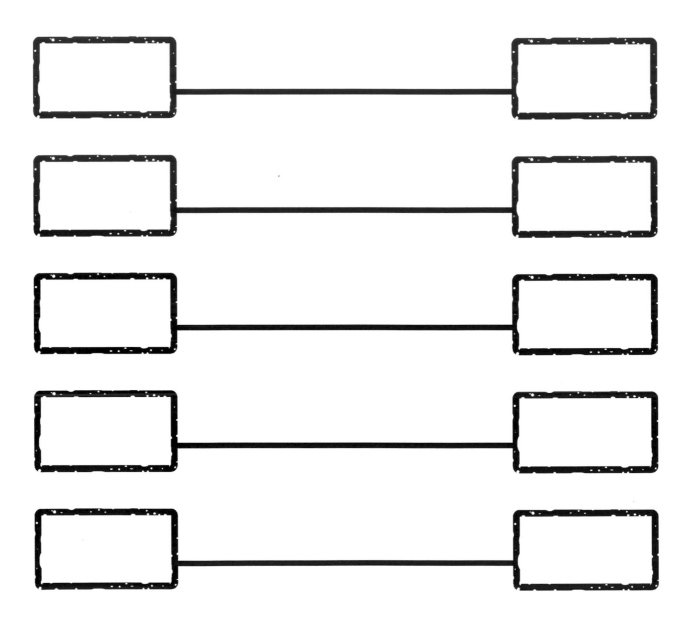

Put a mark on each line to show how near either end you feel you are. Where do teachers, friends and family see you? Choose different colours to show where they would put you on the line.

Put a star on each line to show where you would like to be?

Reputations

A reputation is often the first thing people hear about you. This seems to be particularly the case if you have often been in trouble .... people hear all the bad things about you before they even meet you. This changes the way they see you and what they think about you.

What sort of reputation do you have at school?

What would you like it to be?

What can you start to do today to give yourself a good reputation?

Who needs to notice the improvements you have made in your behaviour for your reputation to begin to change?

    Friends   Other pupils

    Teachers   Head teacher

    Deputy head   Family

How the Future Might Look

This is your Life!

If you were writing the chapter titles for a book about your life so far, what would they be? Thinking about significant events, turning points, failures or achievements may help you.

1.

2.

3.

4.

5.

What would you like the chapters to be called for your future? Think about changes you plan to make, where you see yourself in a year's time, what you would like to do when you leave this school.

6.

7.

8.

9.

10.

Can you think of a
good title for your book?

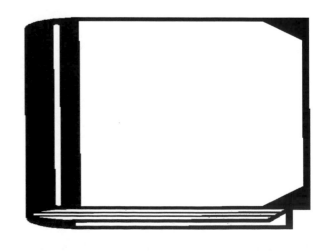

Dream on

If my dreams came true....

Teachers would...	but would not...
My friends would...	but would not...
I would...	but would not...
My family would...	but would not...

What is the first thing you could do to start making your dreams come true?

Who would be the first to notice that things were changing for you?

Rose-tinted specs

Do you know what it means to see life through rose-tinted specs?

What would your life be like through rose-tinted specs?

What could you do to begin to make a difference?

Slice up your day

How big a slice of your day at school do you spend on these activities. You might need to add some more to the list.

* Working
* In lessons you like
* Eating dinner
*

* Messing about in class
* In lessons you don't like
* Talking with your friends
*

Mark the size of the slices on the left-hand pie.

How I spend my day now

How I will soon spend my day

On the right hand pie mark the size of the slices and label them for how you will more usefully spend your day in the future.

Magic Wand

If you could wave a magic wand over the situation in school what would happen?

These things would STOP happening

These things would START happening

These things would happen MORE

Where next?

Where do you want to go after today?
How might you keep on the right road in future?
What will be the signposts to show that you are still on the
right road?

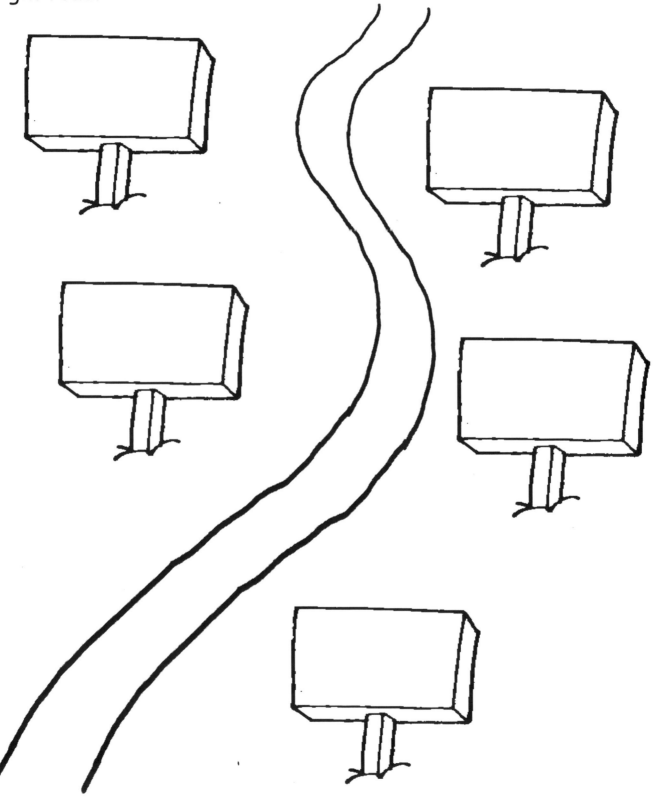

Deal Yourself a Winning Hand

In most card games there is some luck, but there is also skill. If you had all four aces that would be as good a hand as you could usually get. What needs to happen for you to get four aces?

If you had a fifth ace up your sleeve, something you could do to make things almost perfect in school, what would it be?

The Range of Choices for Action

Which way now?

You can make choices about your behaviour and where it will lead you. Think about some of the choices you could make now and put your 4 favourites round this chart.

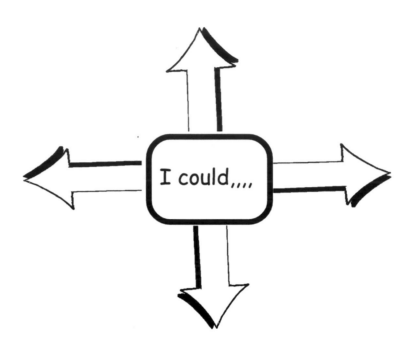

I could,,,,

Which road is it best for you to take now? Do you know why this would be a good choice?

Take the Bull by the Horns

What stops you making the changes you want?	How will you remove the barriers and make a start?

Stuck???

If you are really stuck for a first step to take to make things better think creatively.

Think about what these famous people do and what they are like. What would they suggest for your first step.

The Prime Minister and the Queen

☆ _____

☆ _____

Superman and Bart Simpson

☆ _____

☆ _____

Choose your own two famous characters or real people to help and note down the ideas they might give you.

☆ _____

☆ _____

Give all the new ideas a score out of ten for how much they might help you and write it in the star.

Still Stuck?!

If you are still stuck for a way forward, or feel you would like some more ideas before you make a final decision about what you are going to do, think about how the following objects could give you a new idea. This is called *lateral thinking*. You may have to really rack your brains to come up with something different to try.

A bat

An egg

A tree

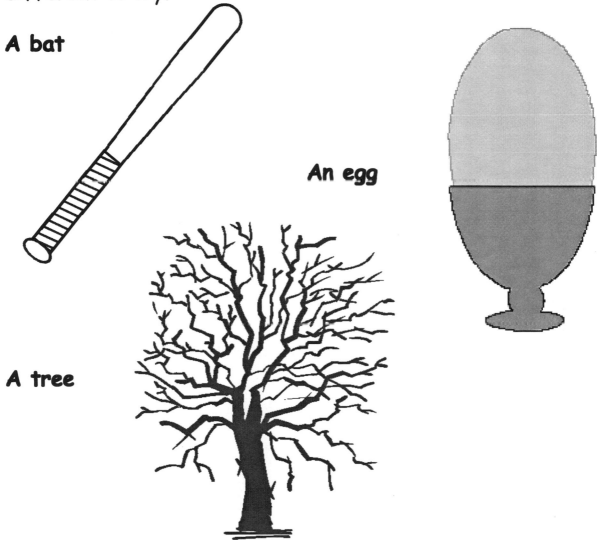

Have you got an idea to work on now? Make some notes so you don't forget.

Pack up your troubles

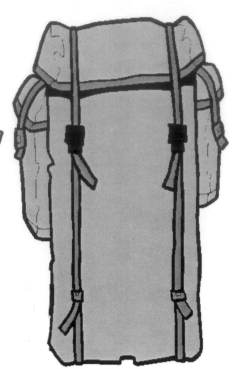

*"Pack up your troubles in your old kit bag
And smile, smile, smile."*

This is the first line of the chorus
of a song many older people will know.

What troubles need to be
packed away in your kit bag to make
you smile, smile, smile?

☺ _____

☺ _____

☺ _____

☺ _____

☺ _____

Mosaic

Tiny pieces of coloured stone or tile were put together by the Romans to make beautiful, intricately patterned floors.

Small pieces of behaviour can also be put together to make a picture of your behaviour in school.

What tiny changes will you make to design a better picture of yourself? Write them in the segments of the mosaic figure.

Juggling

It is hard to keep lots of juggling balls in the air at once and stop them falling all round you. What are all the things you need to do to stop things falling all round you at school?

Write some of them in the juggling balls.

Plaits

Problems are never simple. There are often a number of different strands to them which get knotted together and are difficult to unravel. If you can separate the parts it's often easier to sort them one by one.

Have a think about the situation you are in. What are the different parts that need dealing with? Write them on the strands of this plait.

Are you up a creek ……. without a paddle? If so you may feel well and truly stuck.

If you were in a real canoe you would have to think very hard about how to help yourself even if you could still see the paddle floating just out of reach.

What could you do if you were stuck in a real canoe deep in the Amazon jungle? There might be piranhas in the water, so watch out!

What can you do to get paddling along smoothly again at school? Watch out for the piranha type problems!

Potential Help and pitfals

Banana Skins

What could slip you up on the way to your goal?
Put a possible problem on each segment of the banana skin.

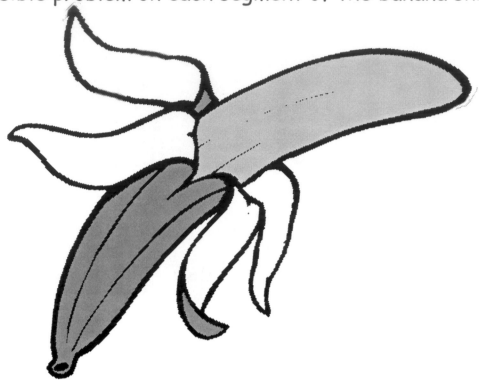

How could you avoid these difficulties?

Who could help you?

Peace summit

World leaders sometimes arrange a peace summit to try to sort out difficulties between countries. Who could help you begin to move forward and resolve your difficulties? Put them round the globe.

Now set the agenda for the meeting. What 3 things should they help you with first?

1.

2.

3.

Every cloud has a silver lining

Things may seem pretty bad at the moment but if you think hard there are bound to be some positive things that can take you forward.

- Perhaps someone is willing to help you sort things out
- Maybe you've now had a chance to talk through your difficulties
- Maybe you are a bit more determined to change now

Think really hard and talk to one of the staff to come up with some other positive and helpful things about the situation you are in.

Make some notes here because it is these positive things that can be the first tiny steps to making life a lot better.

:) _____

:) _____

:) _____

:) _____

Full Speed Ahead

Imagine the speed limit for making changes to your behaviour is 70mph. So 70mph is when you are trying the very, very best you can.

Put in the needle to show how fast are you making changes now.

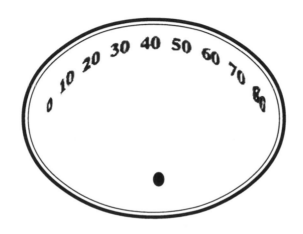

What would help you get you going:

1 mph faster?   ....

....

10 mph faster?   ....

....

Up to the speed limit? ....

....

If at first you don't succeed try, try, try again.

Long, long ago a man called Robert The Bruce was hiding from his enemies. Whilst he was waiting for it to be safe to leave he watched a spider try over and over again to spin the first thread of a web. Eventually the spider was successful and spun a web. Robert The Bruce realised from this he should not give up too easily.

Now things are really hard for you what could you do to try, try, try again?

✹ _____

✹ _____

✹ _____

Who might be able to give you a helping hand, like the spider did for Robert The Bruce? What would you like them to do?

Shark attack

What is in the treasure chest that you really want to get? You can dive for sunken treasure but you must watch out for the sharks which want to stop you getting there.

On the treasure chest write your target. On the sharks write the problems you think you might face.

Obstacle course

An obstacle course can be difficult but when you get to the end you can feel a great sense of achievement. Sorting things out at school will also be challenging but well worth doing.

Write what you would like to achieve on the finish line and label some of the obstacles along the way.

Is there a way to the finish line avoiding some of the obstacles?

Help!!

It's OK to ask for help. You wouldn't be working here now if people weren't willing to help you.

How could these people help you sort things out at school?

Friends

Family

Teachers

Tick one thing in each group that you are going to ask someone to do <u>today</u> to help you.

High-wire act

At the moment you are balancing on a tight-rope. Your behaviour must not let you down. You need to concentrate very hard in order not to make a mistake and fall off. Tight-rope walkers always look ahead to where they are going....they don't look back or down. Fill in on the arrow where you are hoping to go with your behaviour.

There is a safety net in case of accidents. Write the names of some people who can be a safety net and help you to avoid a real disaster.

* _____
* _____
* _____
* _____

Radar

A radar is an early warning system. It helps air traffic controllers guide aeroplanes safely in to land. It would be useful to have a radar system round school to warn you of problems ahead, so you can avoid getting into trouble.

What would be the potential trouble spots you would need to mark? Think about some of these:

- ♦ Times of the day
- ♦ Parts of the building you might be in
- ♦ People you may be with
- ♦ Different lessons
- ♦ How you feel at different times

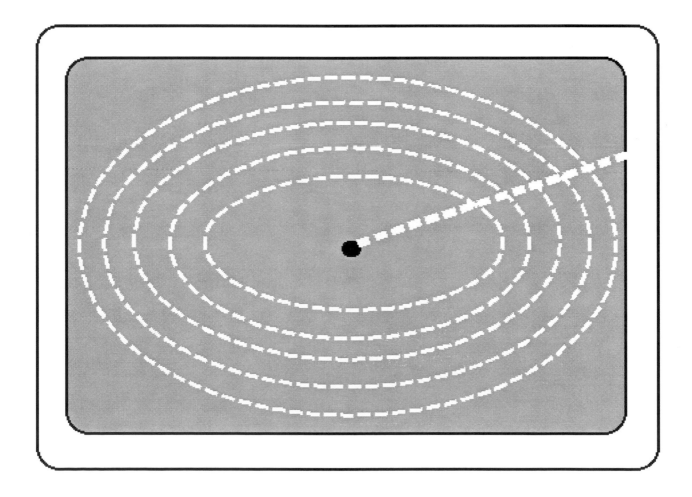

Write some words on the radar to remind you to avoid these difficulties.

Snakes and ladders

In the game of snakes and ladders the snakes drag you down and the ladders help you up to the top. Can you fill in the snakes and ladders on this board with examples from your time in school of the things that help you up and the things that might drag you down.

Section 2

Action Plans

Weight Lifting

Weight-lifters work long and hard to be able to lift the heaviest weights. They set smaller targets along the way to their target lifts.

What steps are you going to take to your target? Make a note of them here. Remember each step will need to be a bit harder than the last one..... but don't make them too hard!

Traffic Lights

Make some notes in each section

STOP

Think about exactly what the problem is.

GET READY

What could you do to move for-ward?

GO

What are you going to do first?

Now go for it!

Sort it

It is often difficult to get started with something that is going to be hard to do. It can help to break the task up into smaller steps.

Note down what you are going to do, and by when, to start helping yourself.

I will _____

    by _____

I will _____

    by _____

I will _____

    by _____

What will be the first thing you will notice that will tell you that things are improving?

Another Brick in the Wall

You could look at this sheet in 2 ways. You might feel that you are trapped behind a brick wall and need to break out.... Or you might feel that the situation you are in is falling apart and you need to build up a solid wall again.

Put an arrow between these walls to show which way you feel you need to move.

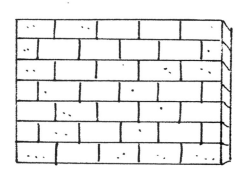   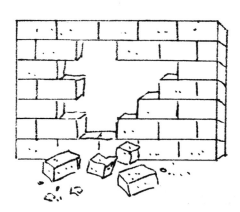

What are <u>you</u> going to do to get started.
Write one action for each brick.

....

....

....

....

How will you know when the wall is as you would want it to be?

Countdown

Start preparing for take-off on your mission by making a ten point plan. Remember that each line of the countdown should be an important part of your overall mission.

My mission is to

10 _____

9 _____

8 _____

7 _____

6 _____

5 _____

4 _____

3 _____

2 _____

1 _____

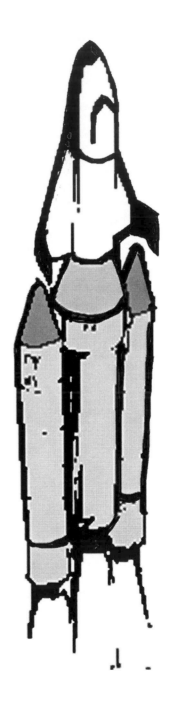

Blast Off !!

Abracadabra

Make a magic spell to help you get rid of your difficulties.
Put all the things you need to do into the cauldron.

What would it be best to do first? Number the ingredients in
the order you plan to put them into action.

Go for Gold

You may feel that you are able to go for gold straight away but it might not be easy. Give yourself some help by awarding yourself a bronze and a silver medal for achievements along the way.

Bronze medal awarded for

....

....

Silver medal awarded for

....

....

Gold medal awarded for

....

....

2 4 6 8
who do we appreciate!

To get people to 'appreciate' you more see if you can come up with:

2 things you really need to change.

4 things people would notice that were different once these changes had been made.

6 things you are going to do this week to begin to make things change.

8 days from now get back together with the person who is supporting you and review how things are progressing.

Cool it

What is the worst your behaviour has been in school?
How hot did it get?
Mark a red line on the thermometer to show this.

Put a blue line to show the calmest and coolest
you have been in school.

What is the temperature now?

What needs to happen to reduce the temperature by

10°

20°

30°

......or back to the coolest it has been

How will you know when things have cooled down
again in school and it is comfortable to be there?

Plan   Do   Review

Your teachers will know all about the 'Plan - Do - Review' cycle. They will often use it to help them improve the way things are in school. You can use it too!

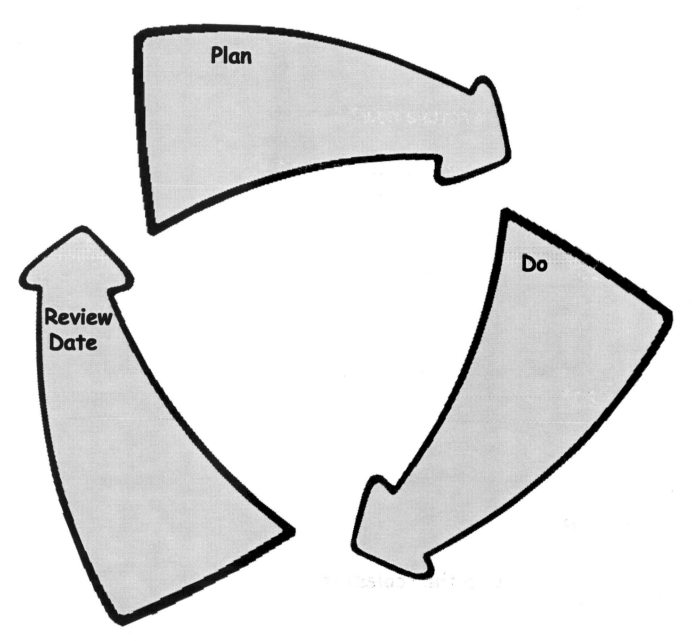

Fill in the **Plan** and **Do** arrows and remember to keep the sheet so that you can use it at the review meeting.

How did you get on? What will you do differently? Will you need a new plan?

The Missing Link

You will already be doing much to improve your behaviour in school but there are probably one or two things you could still do. These may well be the vital missing links!

Fill in the chain by writing in some of the things you are already doing to help yourself. Complete the missing links by adding in two things you could begin to do to make a real improvement in how others see your behaviour.

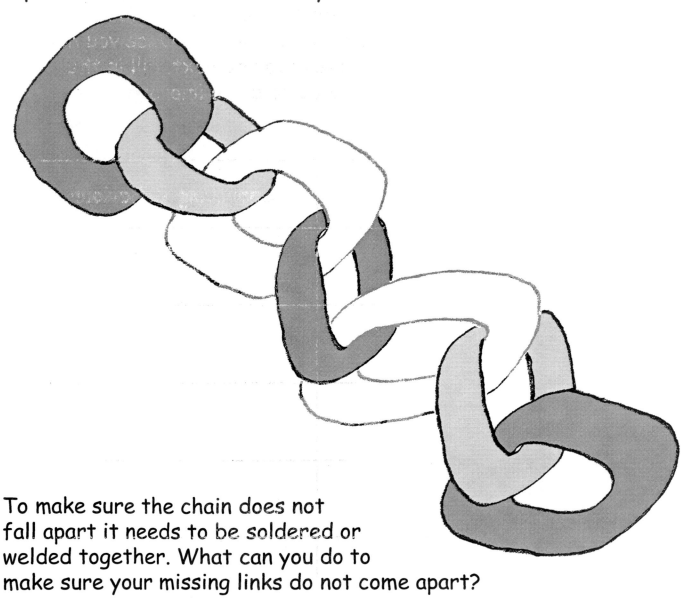

To make sure the chain does not fall apart it needs to be soldered or welded together. What can you do to make sure your missing links do not come apart?

On your bike

Can you remember how hard it was to learn to ride a bike? You will have been a bit wobbly at the start but after lots of practice you will have been able to ride along in a straight line. After even more practice you will have been able to ride round things that got in your way. To learn each new skill you need to be pretty good at the one before.

Improving your behaviour is a bit like learning to ride a bike. If you keep trying you get better and better. Once you have mastered one step you can move onto the next. Fill in the chart to show the things you need to do to improve your behaviour.

Riding a bike	Improving Behaviour
* learn to balance	
* learn to use brakes	
* ride in a wobbly line	
* ride in a straight line	
* ride around obstacles	

Don't run before you can walk

You will not be able to remember learning to walk. It is something that will have taken lots of practice and you will have had lots of help from your family and from things like furniture to hold onto. Each part of the sequence has to be learned before you can do the next. For example you can not walk till you can stand and you can not run until you can walk.

Fill in the flow chart for the steps to make you successful in school.

Learning to walk	Being successful in school
Sit up	
Crawl	
Move round holding on	
Walk holding hands	
Walk alone	
Run, jump, climb	
A successful mover!	**Successful in school**

Tomorrow is the First Day of the rest of your life

Think about the title of this sheet. What do you really want to do with your life? <u>Now</u> is the time to start making those things happen. A time when many people think about their future is on New Years Eve. Resolutions are made for better behaviour in the next year.

It isn't New Years Eve today but you could still make some "New You" resolutions. What would they be?

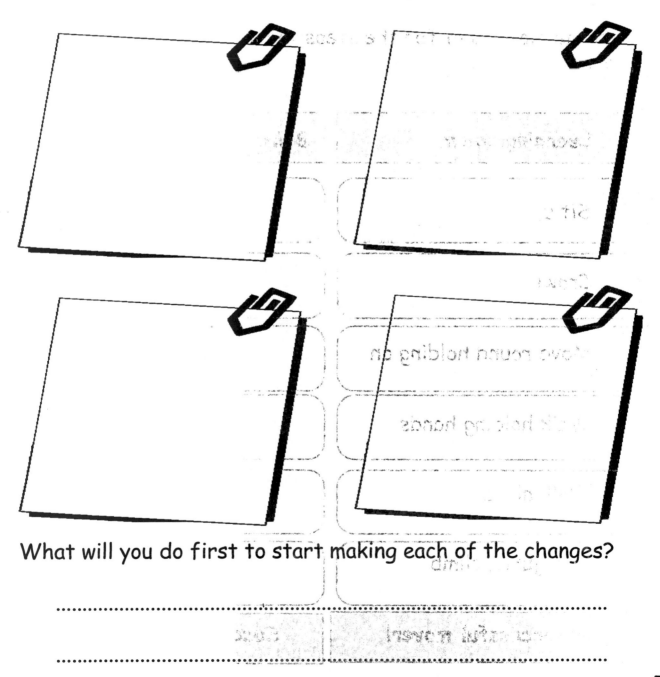

What will you do first to start making each of the changes?

....

....

Look before you leap

Take a careful look at where you plan to go before you dive in. Make sure you know about the hidden difficulties and have a way to deal with them before you encounter them.

This is where I want to go with my behaviour in school.

These are the difficulties I might come across.

These are ways I could avoid the problems happening at all.

These are ways I could deal with the problems that do arise.

Experiment

When you write about a scientific experiment you put information under these headings:

- **Hypothesis**- what you think might happen as a result of your experiment?
- **Method**- this describes exactly what you did.
- **Results**- this section describes what happened.
- **Conclusion**- here you say what you have learned from your experiment.

Try this as a way of experimenting with your behaviour to see what happens if you change some of the things you do.

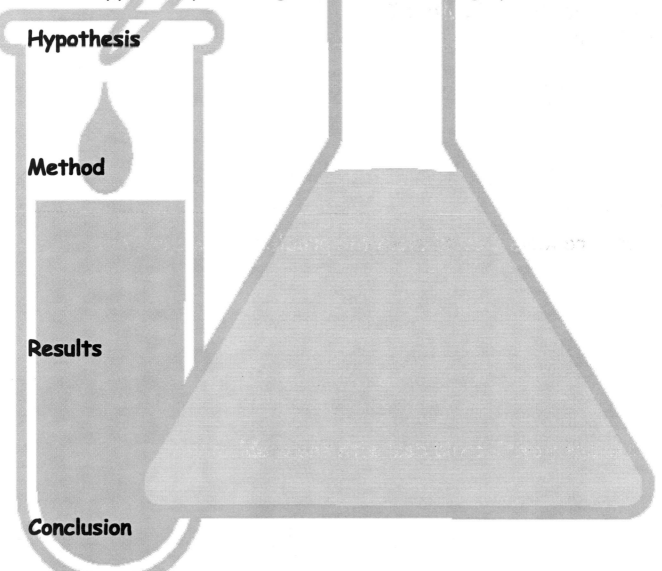

Hypothesis

Method

Results

Conclusion

Marathon run

Running 26 miles takes a lot of preparation and determination. If you trained for a marathon you would run nearly every day, exercise all your muscles, eat a healthy diet and get lots of rest too. You would set yourself targets and build up to them. Improving your behaviour in school will also take preparation and determination. Decide on the milestones along your marathon route to your chosen finish line.

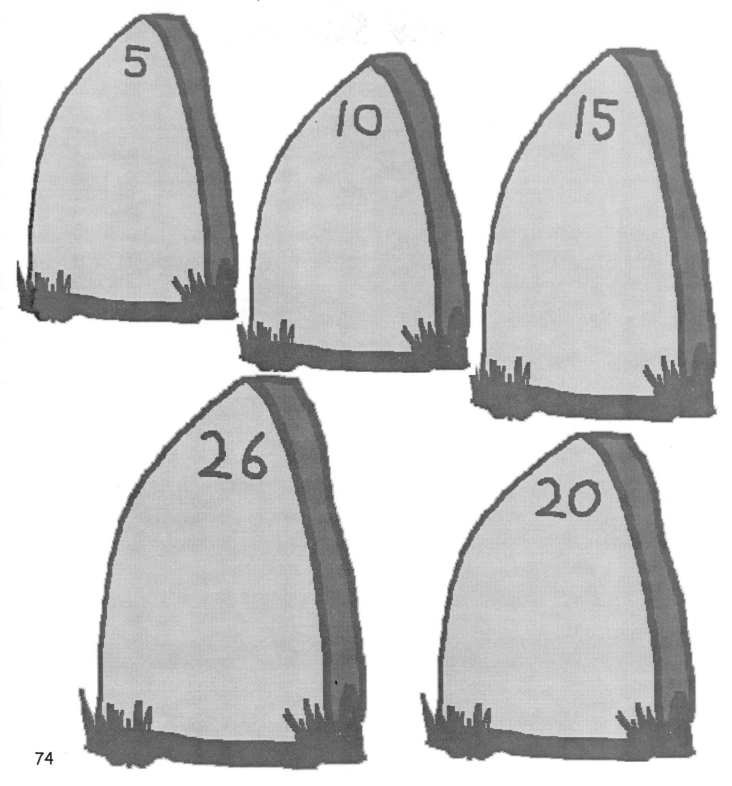

Review Sheets

Pit stop

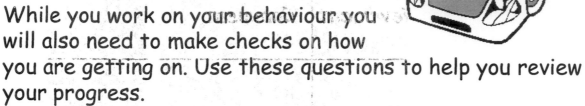

Grand Prix racing drivers get called into the pits part way through a race to check tyres and engines and to fill up with fuel ready for the next laps.

While you work on your behaviour you will also need to make checks on how you are getting on. Use these questions to help you review your progress.

Have you stuck to your plan?

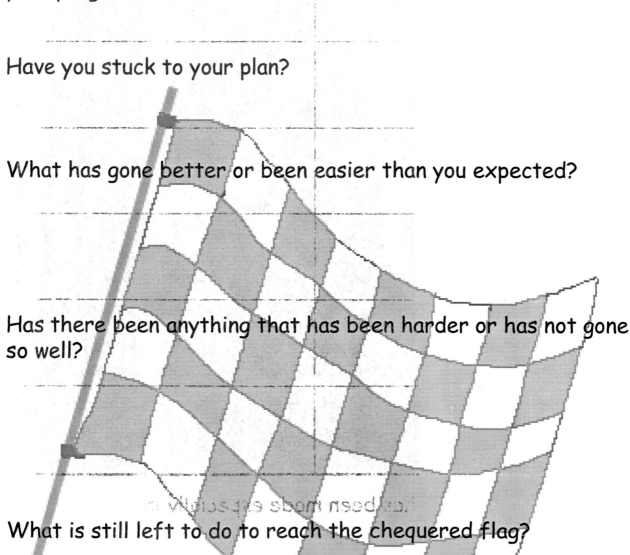

What has gone better or been easier than you expected?

Has there been anything that has been harder or has not gone so well?

What is still left to do to reach the chequered flag?

Reports!!

Write your own report of how you are getting on with improving your behaviour in lessons or around school. Give yourself a mark for effort and for achievement and write a comment if you think you need to.

Subject	Effort	Achievement	Comment

Overall good progress has been made especially in

More effort needs to be made with

How am I doing?

Choose the areas you are going to review. Write them in the boxes along the bottom. Fill in the bar chart to show how you are doing.

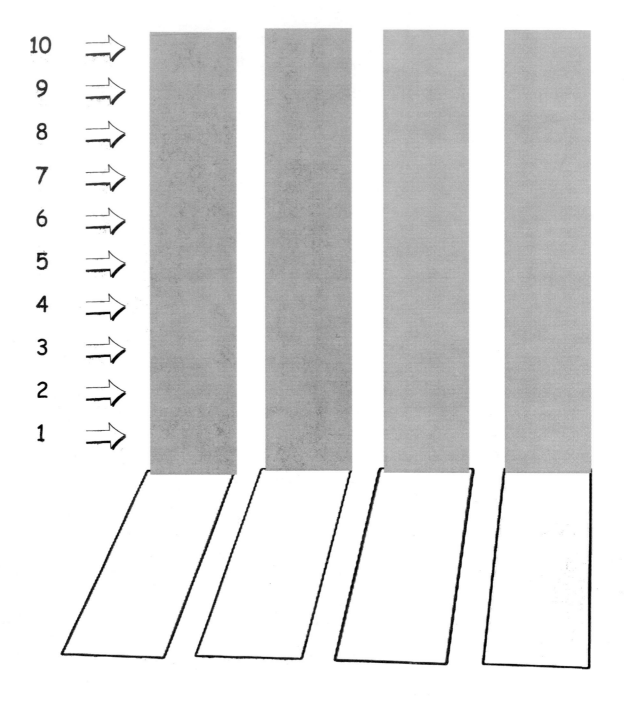

How could you improve your scores before a future review?